A Long Night For Mr. Dennis

A LONG NIGHT FOR MR. DENNIS

Mr. Dennis

Nancy J. Carlson

Illustrated by Mariya Stoyanova

Mill City Press, Inc.
2301 Lucien Way #415
Maitland, FL 32751
407.339.4217
www.millcitypress.net

Paperback ISBN-13: 978-1-6628-1016-9

Ebook ISBN-13: 978-1-6628-1017-6

In memory of my Lovebucket,
my Dreamboat, my Dennis.

Mr. Dennis is a Boston Terrier. His fur is white and black and he has a black spot on the top of his head.

His owner and best friend, Nancy, calls this spot his on/ off button. Well, that button did not turn him off on the eve of July 4th as Nancy had hoped.

You see, Mr. Dennis is frightened by loud noises. That night in his home town of Ticonderoga, NY, many fireworks burst into the sky for their Best 4th in the North celebration.

These loud fireworks scared him, so he pushed open the door and started to run toward the woods.

After some time he stopped, looked side to side, then back and forth only to realize he was lost! He sniffed the cool night air for some sign of home but the smells were so different!

6

8

Just then something moved in the bushes ahead so he sniffed the air again. "Hmm, smells like Saga, my German Sheppard sister," he thought. "Hello, is that you Saga?"

9

"Grr, Grr," was the answer he heard not from Saga but from a coyote. "Mr. Coyote, do you know where Nancy is?" Mr. Dennis asked.

"GRR, GRR," growled the coyote much louder this time.
Mr. Dennis yelped then quickly turned to run away.

He then saw some twinkling lights up ahead.
"Oh good," he thought, "maybe those lights are coming from my house!" As he moved closer the lights started to move away.

He then thought about his backyard that twinkled with lights just like these and remembered Nancy's saying they came from Fireflies. Realizing he was not near home made him sad so he continued on his way.

He turned to run and bumped right into a tree stump.

16

Feeling a little dazed he stopped to rest a little, closed his teary eyes, and fell asleep.

18

A few hours passed and Mr. Dennis woke to the sound of chirping birds as the morning light shone through the tree branches.

His eyes felt a little better but they started to tear as he began to cry. "Nancy, where are you?"

A Barred Owl perched in a tree above him heard the crying.
"Whooo, whooo are you?" the owl hooted.

22

"My name is Dennis, do you know where Nancy is?" "What is a Nancy?" the owl asked. "She is a people and my best friend. I can't find her," he replied.

The owl took flight and motioned for Mr. Dennis to follow. She led him to a house at the edge of the forest.

After thanking the owl, Mr. Dennis walked up to the house. A lady came out, looked down at him, and asked, "Aww, are you lost?" Now smelly, puffy eyed and tired, he weakly replied, "Do you know where Nancy is?"

27

The nice lady called the Dog Warden to help.

"Poor puppy," the warden said, "looks like you had a long night." He first checked for any injuries before wrapping Mr. Dennis in a soft blanket. The warden thanked the nice lady, laid him in the truck, and drove away.

31

Nancy and her family had been making calls and walking around the neighborhood all through the night hoping they would find Mr. Dennis. The warden heard about these calls and drove straight to Nancy's house.

The whole family ran out to greet Mr. Dennis and to thank the warden. Smelly and all, Mr. Dennis was hugged and kissed by the whole family. Their beloved pet happily sighed, snuggled, and kissed them all back.

CPSIA information can be obtained
at www.ICGtesting.com
Printed in the USA
LVHW072110280521
688852LV00007B/94

9 781662 810169